This is MORE than just a LARGE [...] Colouring Book and Devoti[...]

SECTION 1: Contains my own original p[...] inspiration behind them. It is designed [...] [...]urage meditation on the painting titles and associ[...]ed scriptures, allowing God to speak through your colouring experience. Due to artistic limitations, the drawings are not exact copies of the original paintings but are, nevertheless, close representations. There are adjacent greyscale pictures to assist with shading...*and to help improve colour-blending skills.* By using this option, you can capture the details of the original artwork and bring your picture to life. As a colour guide, you can find photos of my original paintings on the back cover. However, each drawing is *for your own personal interpretation - there are NO rules to follow!!!*

SECTION 2: Contains additional scriptures and drawings for you to simply enjoy colouring and meditate on.

All drawings have been left blank on the reverse side (apart from the gift label) to avoid possible bleed-through from colouring. There are also 'CUT-LINES' allowing pictures to be detached from the book for framing or gifting, if desired. I have paraphrased some of the scriptures to comply with copyright requirements.

SECTION 3: Includes three personal stories, an invitation and prayer, dedications, and details of how to locate my other publications.

The LARGE PRINT in this colouring book provides clear, easy-to-read text, making it ideal for a variety of age groups...*but particularly helpful for seniors!* It is designed to encourage relaxation and a deepened relationship with God...*to help you spend time **WITH HIM** rather than just learning **ABOUT HIM!!!***

It can also be used to spread the Good News of Jesus Christ to all those open to the Christian faith...

Contents

SECTION 1: A Collection of 16 Drawings (based on original paintings). Each set of four pages includes:
About the Painting & Thoughts to Ponder + Greyscale Painting + Drawing to Colour + Bleed Page + Gift Label

SECTION 2: A Collection of 16 Scripture-based Drawings, Pages 067-098: Each set of two pages includes:
A Scripture & Drawing to Colour + Bleed Page + Gift Label

SECTION 3:

First published April 2021 by Books to Bless

Contact: **rita.artthatspeaks@gmail.com** / ⓞ Instagram: rita.artthatspeaks OR bookstobless)

ISBN: 9798741026267

Painting 01: 'Be Free'

About the painting...

The preacher punched his clenched fist forward; "Unforgiveness" he exclaimed! My spirit gasped, "That's a painting!" – *the thrust* of *his words pierced deep into my being!*

I based this painting on the preacher's clenched fist. Chains speak of the prison that things such as unforgiveness can keep us in, so it seemed fitting to combine both things into the picture. I wanted to express the freedom of forgiveness in the second part of the painting; hence the unfolding hand and the joyful daisies on a blanket of fresh green grass. The Bible says in John 8, verses 32 & 36, *'Then you will know the truth, and the truth will set you free.'* and *'So if the Son sets you free, you will be free indeed.'* These scriptures fitted perfectly!

Thoughts to Ponder...

When we hold onto unforgiveness we actually keep *ourselves* in a prison...*NOT the person that has done the wrong!* We can become bitter, and it can also affect *our health*. We need to activate our free will and choose to forgive. That doesn't mean what they did was ok, and it doesn't mean we will necessarily trust that person. *Trust needs to be earned!!!* But, when we think about **how much** we've been forgiven by God, through Jesus, then whatever they've done seems incredibly small.

Why not take a moment, and in the silence of your heart give to The Lord 'Whatever Binds You', be it fear, failure, unforgiveness, jealousy, shame, envy, your past, your future, fill in the blank .... 'Let It Go' *'BE FREE'!!!*

'Be Free'

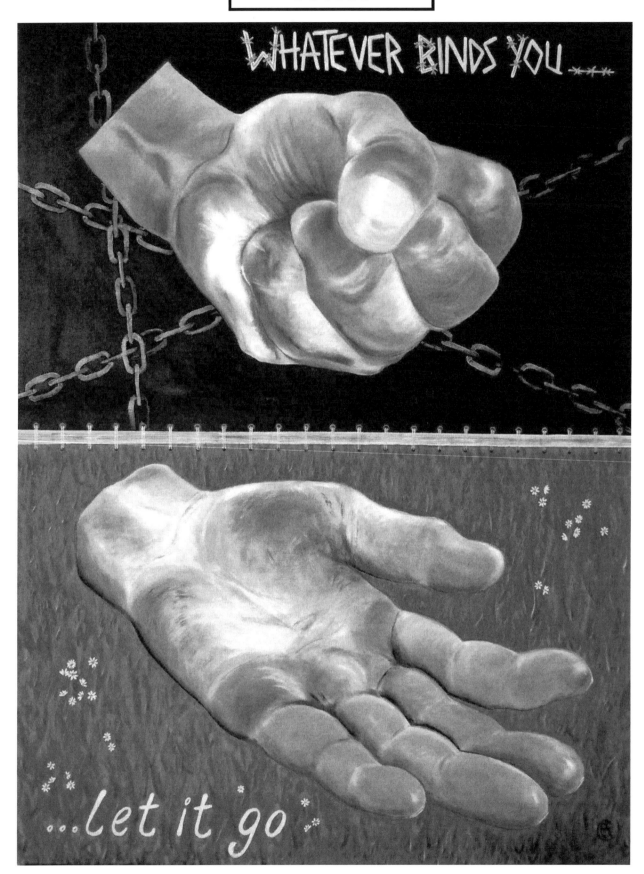

'**Then you will know the truth, and the truth will set you free.**' and '**So if the Son sets you free, you will be free indeed.**' *(John 8:32 & 36)*

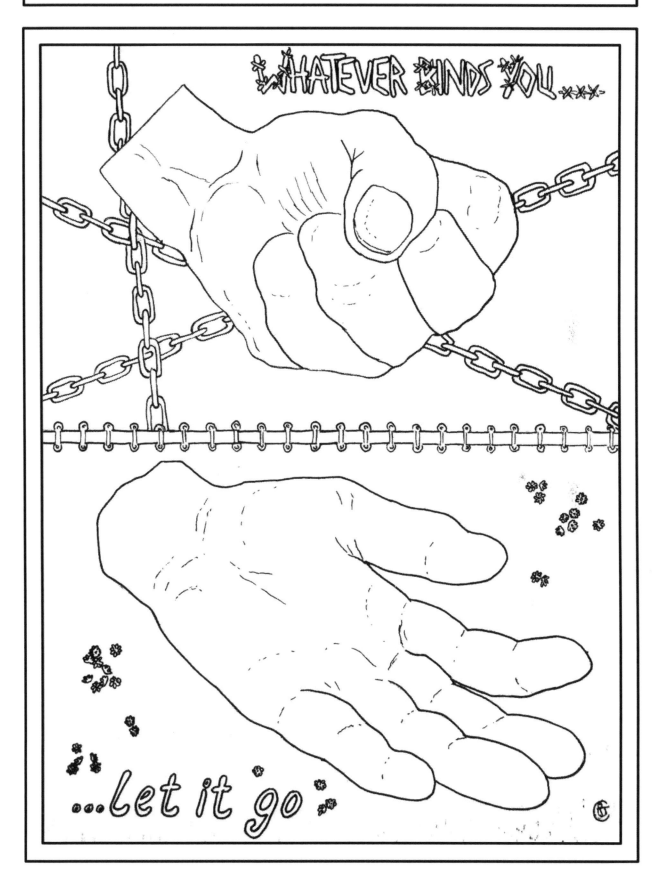

Date: ___ / ___ / _____ To: _____ From: _____

A colouring gift from Me to You...taken from the book:

CHRISTIAN COLOURING BOOK **LARGE PRINT** DEVOTIONAL...*and more!!!* (Volume 1)

By **ART THAT SPEAKS** – Rita Clark (*found on Amazon*)

Painting 02: **'Searching For You'**

About the Painting...

This painting is in the style of another of my paintings called 'Seeking His Presence'. I loved the colours I used in the first one, but this time I wanted to do a second version to compliment the décor in my home. I chose peachy oranges and bluey greens, and this did the job perfectly. The finished work graced the wall in my dining room for many years...*until I decided to re-decorate!*

Thoughts to Ponder...

Who is searching for whom? Have you found God, and has He found you? Or, are you still searching for Him and He for you? The Bible says in Jeremiah 29, verse 13, *'You will seek Me and find Me when you search for Me with all your heart'.* At every level of relationship there is always more. He invites you to come closer to Him today...w*ill you?*

He sees you and knows you. He knit you together in your mother's womb. Even if you felt unplanned or unwanted ...**He wanted you!!!** He chose you before time began. In the beginning, when God created the world, **He already knew you** and chose YOU to walk with Him...*side by side, together!*

He sees your heart. He knows your every thought. What are you thinking right now?

The mist is clearing, it's time for you both to meet! Perhaps even for the first time!! He's waiting...*He's waiting for YOU!!!*

NOW is the moment, He beckons you 'Come'...

Will you?

'Searching For You'

'You will seek Me and find Me when you search for Me with all your heart.'
(Jeremiah 29:13)

Searching For You

Date: ___ / ___ / _____ To: _____ From: _____

A colouring gift from Me to You...taken from the book:

CHRISTIAN COLOURING BOOK **LARGE PRINT** DEVOTIONAL...*and more!!!* (Volume 1)

By **ART THAT SPEAKS** – Rita Clark (*found on Amazon*)

Painting 03: **'You Are Not Alone'**

About the Painting...

I wanted to paint a picture that would bring comfort and express how much a sunset means to me. *This is the reason why...* In 1986, when at my lowest ebb, I heard the audible voice of God tell me that 'He, God, puts His arms around me *through the sunset*, open fields, and my baby's smile!' *In that moment, my life changed forever...*

I love being in the great outdoors. Open spaces and the beauty of God's amazing creation *always* sooth my heart. When I stand listening to the sound of crashing waves breaking onto a vast deserted beach, I'm comforted. So, I decided to paint a sunset with a wonderful seascape! I also wanted to place an image of Jesus next to a person that thought they were totally alone. *I feel like I achieved all I hoped for in this painting...*

Thoughts to Ponder...

God puts His arms around us in many ways. He is *always* ready to reveal Himself to us. Until that moment, when I heard His audible voice, I didn't even know God existed. *But that didn't mean He wasn't there!* He *was* there – I just didn't realise it until, in desperation, I cried out to Him! It says in the Bible Hebrews 13, verse 5b, 'I will NEVER leave you or forsake you'.

Perhaps you're thinking *'He's not with me.'* Even so, He IS with you, and He wants to comfort you...*He LOVES you!*

Why not turn your heart toward Him right now...
and in THIS moment, you too can realise,
'You Are Not Alone'!!!

'You Are Not Alone'

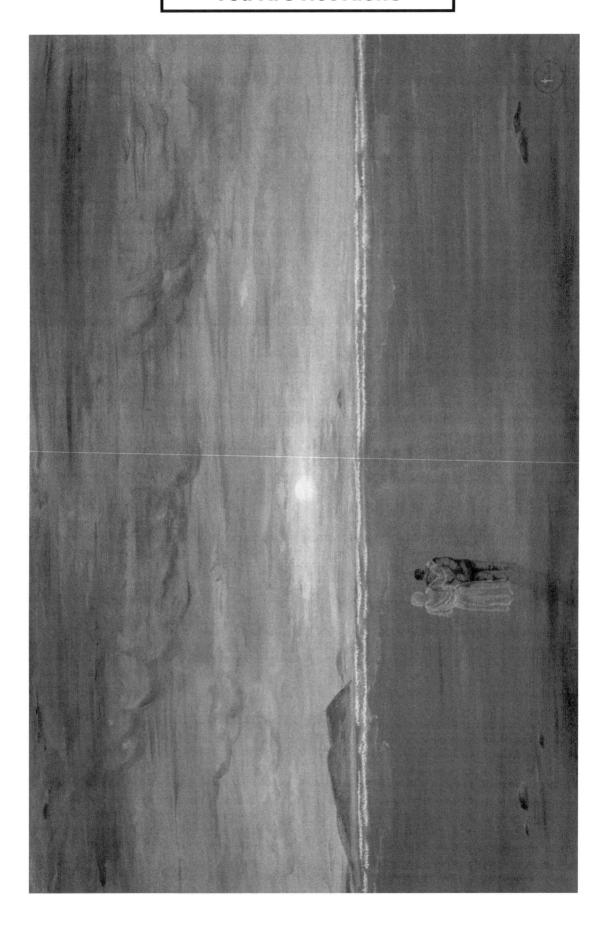

'You Are Not Alone'

' *I will never leave you or forsake you.*'

(Hebrews 13:5b)

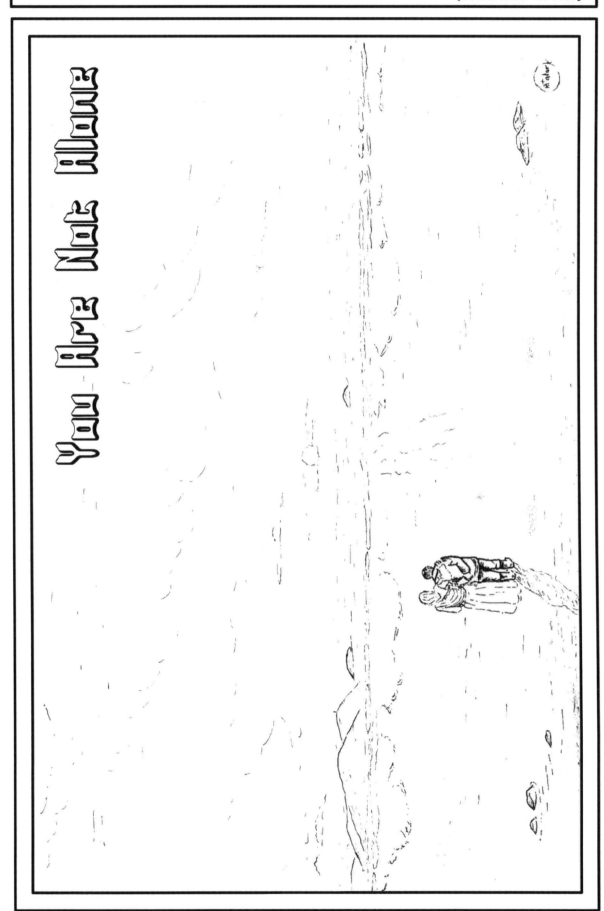

' *I will never leave you or forsake you.*'

(Hebrews 13:5b)

Date: ___ / ___ / _____ To: _____ From: _____

*A colouring gift from **Me to You**...taken from the book:*

CHRISTIAN COLOURING BOOK **LARGE PRINT** DEVOTIONAL...*and more!!!* (Volume 1)

By **ART THAT SPEAKS** – Rita Clark (*found on Amazon*)

Painting 04: 'Have FAITH'

About the painting...

This is my second painting based on this imagery. With the original one, I wanted to create a picture of a seascape with a big sky. I love sunsets and that was my immediate thought, but I'd already painted several others using that expression; this time I wanted to do something different. When I thought about painting the moon and stars on a velvety black sky, together with waves breaking into the silence of a peaceful shoreline, my heart leapt...*so that's what I did!*

I wanted to use this second painting to encourage us to think about faith. The Bible passage that came to mind was Hebrews 11, verse 6, where it says, *'And without faith it is impossible to please God, because anyone who comes to Him must believe that He exists, and that He rewards those who earnestly seek Him.'* To please God, we need to 'Have FAITH'...*so it felt right to make these two words the focal point of this painting!*

Thoughts to Ponder...

Let me encourage you to imagine this scene – thousands of stars, twinkling against the backdrop of the night sky; the sound of waves lapping on the seashore; shimmering flecks of moonlight dancing on the water and reflecting onto glistening wet sand; the smell of saltiness in the air. The perfect atmosphere to savour the presence of our Creator and embrace the stunning world we live in. God wants us to 'Have FAITH' in the knowledge of His existence. *He longs to reward us with His presence!!!*

Why not be still in Father's presence right now?
Quieten your mind, and listen to what
He whispers into your heart...

Remember, above ALL, HE is our great reward!!!

'Have FAITH'

'**And without faith it is impossible to please God because anyone who comes to Him must believe that He exists, and that He rewards those who earnestly seek Him.'** (Hebrews 11:6)

Date: ___ / ___ / _____ To: _____ From: _____

A colouring gift from Me to You...taken from the book:

CHRISTIAN COLOURING BOOK **LARGE PRINT** DEVOTIONAL...*and more!!!* (Volume 1)

By **ART THAT SPEAKS** – Rita Clark (*found on Amazon*)

Painting 05: 'Anointed One'

About the Painting...

I wanted to paint a picture to compliment my home décor, and I wanted it to be a picture of Jesus on the cross. I was awake in the early hours, and the cream canvas with shafts of light on it stared back at me from across the room. I was afraid. How could I possibly paint a picture of my Lord? Gingerly, and using very watery paint, I started to sketch out Jesus...*and loved what was happening!* It made my heart skip, so I stopped right there. I kept it simple; my Jesus was ascending into glory!!!

Thoughts to Ponder...

The Bible says in John 3, verses 16-17, *'For God so loved the world that He gave His one and only Son, so that WHOEVER believes in Him will not die but will have eternal life. For God did not send His Son into the world to condemn the world, but that the world through Him might be saved.'*

Do you realise that **YOU** are one of the **'WHOEVER'???** Good! Now you can also realise that Jesus died to save YOU...**Yes, YOU!!!**

Are you *already* walking in the knowledge of His love and forgiveness? If so, praise God...*I'm so glad we're in the same family!* But if not, then God is offering you the opportunity to enter His love and forgiveness *RIGHT NOW!*

Both He and I would love to welcome YOU
into the family of God. *Will you come?*

I can promise you this...*you'll be so glad you did!!!*

'Anointed One'

> *'For God so loved the world that He gave His one and only Son,*
> *so that WHOEVER believes in Him will not die*
> *but will have eternal life.'*   *(John 3:16)*

Anointed One

Date: ___ / ___ / _____ To: _____ From: _____

A colouring gift from Me to You...taken from the book:

CHRISTIAN COLOURING BOOK **LARGE PRINT** DEVOTIONAL...*and more!!!* (Volume 1)

By **ART THAT SPEAKS** – Rita Clark (*found on Amazon*)

Painting 06: **'Yonder Hope'**

About the Painting...

I wanted to paint with a simple colour palette and I chose pale blue. I love mountains so that's what I painted. The scripture on my heart was Psalm 121, verses 1-2, *'I lift up my eyes to the mountains...where does my help come from? My help comes from the Lord, the Maker of heaven and earth'*. At the time, I needed that help to come to my rescue...*yet it seemed to be distant*. However, as always, it came...*God ALWAYS helps me!* It seemed fitting to call the finished work, 'Yonder Hope'.

My late Nan's favourite colour was blue, and it is to her – *and the senior generation generally* – that I dedicate this book. On page 106, you can read about something that happened between my nan and I a few days before she died.

Thoughts to Ponder...

I find the best place to run when I'm in need, feeling isolated or hurting, is into the open arms of Jesus. It's soooooooooo comforting to know that when everything in the world seems disagreeable, I can turn to the Lord for His strength. *And so can you my friend...'Yonder Hope' is closer than you think!*

Why not take a few moments to consider this?
You'll be so glad you did!!!

'Yonder Hope'

'I lift up my eyes to the mountains...where does my help come from?
My help comes from the Lord, the Maker of heaven and earth.'
(Psalm 121:1-2)

Date: ___ / ___ / _____ To: _____ From: _____

*A colouring gift from **Me to You***...taken from the book:

CHRISTIAN COLOURING BOOK **LARGE PRINT** DEVOTIONAL...*and more!!!* (Volume 1)

By **ART THAT SPEAKS** – Rita Clark (*found on Amazon*)

Painting 07: **'PEACE...Be With You'**

About the Painting...

I chose the word PEACE as the focal point of this painting, then considered how I could convey all I wanted to say in a simple image. The colours needed to be comforting, not loud or joyful, and have an atmosphere of stillness in the air. As I thought about it, I decided a peaceful sunset with a motionless boat reflecting on still waters would convey that message perfectly...*so that's what I painted!*

Thoughts to Ponder...

To express this painting, I chose a scripture found in the Bible in John 14, verse 27,

> *'Peace I leave with you; My peace I give you.*
> *I do not give to you as the world gives.*
> *Do not let your hearts be troubled*
> *and do not be afraid.'*

The world is full of anxiety and anguish, but Jesus tells us 'DO NOT let your heart be troubled'. As we choose to place our problems and the cares of this world into HIS hands...*we receive HIS peace in exchange!*

It is my sincere hope that as you spend time
in HIS presence, colouring this picture,
you will know HIS deep peace in YOUR heart!!!

'PEACE...Be With You.'

'PEACE Be With You'

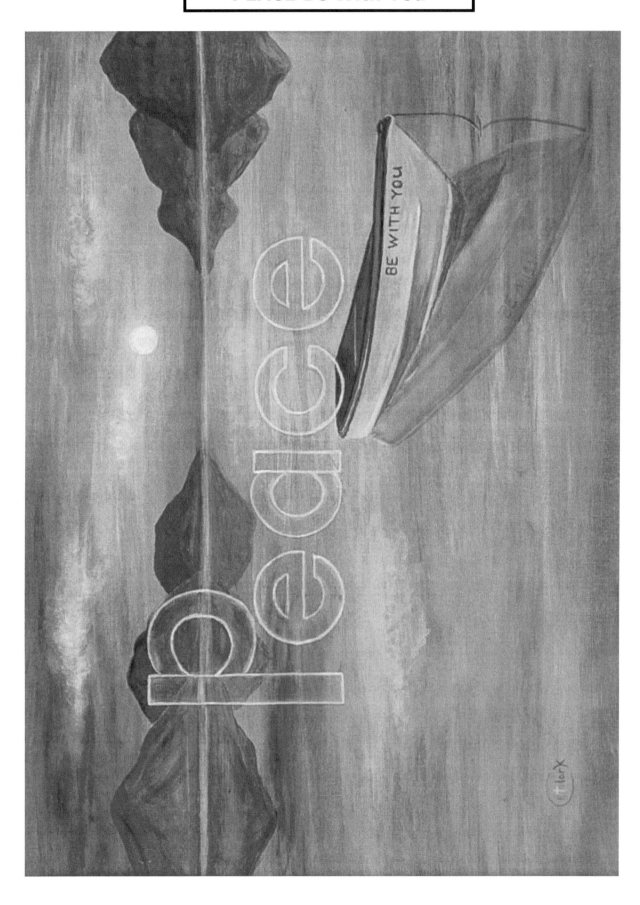

'*Peace I leave with you; My peace I give you. I do not give to you as the world gives. Do not let your hearts be troubled and do not be afraid.*'

(John 14:27)

'*Peace I leave with you; My peace I give you. I do not give to you as the world gives. Do not let your hearts be troubled and do not be afraid.*'

(John 14:27)

Date: ___ / ___ / _____ To: _____ From: _____

A colouring gift from Me to You...taken from the book:

CHRISTIAN COLOURING BOOK **LARGE PRINT** DEVOTIONAL...*and more!!!* (Volume 1)

By **ART THAT SPEAKS** – Rita Clark (*found on Amazon*)

Painting 08: **'He Loves You'**

About the Painting...

The challenge before me was to use allegory to turn a scripture into a painting. (An allegory uses one image to symbolize another to convey its message.) The scripture was Matthew 26, verses 26-28, *'Jesus took the bread, gave thanks and gave it to His disciples saying, "Take and eat, this is My body." Then He took the cup, gave thanks and offered it to them saying, "Drink from it all of you. This is My blood of the new covenant, which is poured out for many for the forgiveness of sins."'*

When taking the bread and wine – *usually known as Holy Communion or Eucharist* – wine is the symbol of Jesus' poured-out blood. The red hearts in this painting represent both His blood, and His love being poured out for all humanity. Purple speaks of His royalty and majesty. Yellow is for His light and glory, and the swish-movement shows His power. The person clothed in white represents the cleansing and sanctification purchased by His blood. The pedestal signifies that God sees the individual person as special. I wanted the bread to be a normal well-baked loaf, so it made sense to paint it in a rusty-tan colour. To bring clarity to the picture and bring the whole image together, I added the nail-pierced hands of Jesus Himself.

Thoughts to Ponder...

Jesus loves **YOU** this much!!!
He wants a deep, loving relationship with ***YOU*...**

If you haven't already done so, will you receive Him now?

‘He Loves You’

Jesus took bread saying, *"Take and eat; this is My body."* Then He took a cup saying, *"Drink from it, all of you. This is My blood of the new covenant, poured out for the forgiveness of sins."* (Matt 26:26-28)

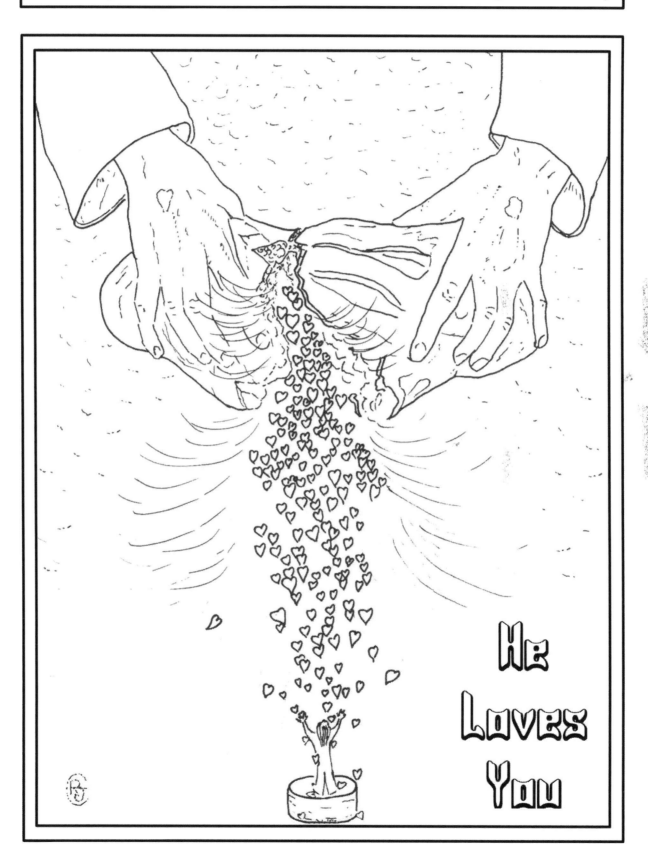

Date: ___ / ___ / _____ To: _____ From: _____

A colouring gift from Me to You...taken from the book:

CHRISTIAN COLOURING BOOK **LARGE PRINT** DEVOTIONAL...*and more!!!* (Volume 1)

By **ART THAT SPEAKS** – Rita Clark (*found on Amazon*)

Painting 09: **'He Knew the Cost'**

About the Painting...

This painting has *two* subjects; both touch the core of my being – God's Son (Jesus Christ) and the sunset!

In 1986, uncertain of His existence, I asked God a question. "How can I love you with all my heart, with all my soul, and with all my mind? I need to *feel* someone's arms around me." In that very moment, He answered me with an audible voice...*and my life changed forever!* One of the things He said was how He put His arms around me through the sunset – *see page 101 for this part of my testimony!*

In the Bible in Matthew 7, verses 7-8, it says: *'Ask and it will be given to you; seek and you will find; knock and the door will be opened to you. For everyone who asks receives; he who seeks finds; and to him who knocks, the door will be opened.'*

With a sincere and desperate heart, I had unwittingly asked God a question. As we can see in this verse from the Bible, God keeps His Word. *HE ANSWERED ME!!! He ALWAYS keeps His Word!*

Thoughts to Ponder...

Jesus 'Knew the Cost'...the price He willingly paid on the cross for our sin. *HE made the way for us to KNOW the Father!!!*

Look carefully at the greyscale picture of this painting, or at the coloured version (on the back cover); can you see Jesus? A lot of people miss Him at first...*this also happens in life!* We often don't see Him...*but He is ALWAYS there!!!*

Look for Jesus today...
He's waiting for YOU to find Him!!!

'He Knew the Cost.'

'Ask and it will be given to you; seek and you will find; knock and the door will be opened to you. For everyone who asks receives; he who seeks finds, and to him who knocks, the door will be opened.' (Matthew 7:7-8)

We Know the Lost

Date: ___ / ___ / _____ To: _____ From: _____

A colouring gift from Me to You...taken from the book:

CHRISTIAN COLOURING BOOK **LARGE PRINT** DEVOTIONAL...*and more!!!* (Volume 1)

By **ART THAT SPEAKS** – Rita Clark (*found on Amazon*)

Painting 10: **'Enter His Rest'**

About the Painting...

Sometimes I create paintings to complement the décor in my home, and that's what I did here. I love England's autumn colours, and these were the ideal colours for the room I had in mind. I also wanted to remind myself of the Father's precious gift of His Son Jesus. The scene needed to communicate a peaceful atmosphere, one that would draw me to 'Enter His Rest' as I looked at it. *And that's what so often happens when I glance at this painting...*

Thoughts to Ponder...

As people, we tend to spend too much time worrying about what *might* happen, when most of the time it doesn't! *So, why worry about it?*

Worry often leads to stress, and it's been proven that this works against good health in our mind and body...*so why destroy our own health??*

The Bible tells us to, *'Cast our cares upon Jesus because He cares for us!'* So let's aim to do just that and live a freer life! Jesus tells us in Matthew 6, verse 25, *"Therefore I tell you, do not worry about your life, what you will eat or drink; or about your body, what you will wear. Is not life more than food, and the body more than clothes?"* God will take care of those things when we place our trust in Him...

Worry won't get us the peace we hunger for...
ONLY accepting the finished work of the cross
and ALL Jesus has *already provided* does that!!!

*...and through the cross we **'Enter His Rest'!!!***

Will YOU choose to place YOUR trust in Jesus TODAY?

'Enter His Rest'

"Therefore I tell you, do not worry about your life, what you will eat or drink, or about your body, what you will wear. Is not life more than food, and the body more than clothes?"   *(Matt 6:25)*

Enter His Rest

Date: ___ / ___ / _____ To: _____ From: _____

A colouring gift from Me to You...taken from the book:

CHRISTIAN COLOURING BOOK **LARGE PRINT** DEVOTIONAL...*and more!!!* (Volume 1)

By **ART THAT SPEAKS** – Rita Clark (*found on Amazon*)

Painting 11: 'God Has Made A Way'

About the Painting...

For the purpose of this colouring book I decided to change the painting's title! I usually call it 'God Will Make A Way', but artistic license allows me the freedom to make changes. 😊 😊 I initially painted it after praying for someone; God showed me this simple image in my mind...*and that person's prayer was answered! God made a way for him!!!*

When it was time to create the painting, I decided to keep it simple, just as the image had been the night God gave it to me; I wanted to use a limited palette. Because Moses had parted the Red Sea, red would have been the obvious choice, but that didn't appeal to me; neither did blue even though sea is often that colour. So, I decided to compromise and use a bluey-mauve, which I preferred. When I looked at a photo of the final artwork its appearance was completely mauve...*and I liked it!* So that's the shade I now use in my illustrations.

Thoughts to Ponder...

In the Old Testament (the first half of the Bible) we read that God rescued the Israelites from the advancing Egyptian army. There was nowhere to go...*but God parted the Red Sea for them!* Then, they were able to advance across into the Promised Land on dry ground! In the New Testament (the second half of the Bible) 'God Has Made A Way' for us to enter heaven through the death, burial and resurrection of Jesus Christ, who died on the cross for us. This was God's gift to us *ALL.* He sent His Son into the world to save it. In John 14, verse 6, it says, *'Jesus said, "I AM the Way, the Truth and the Life, no one comes to the Father except through me."'*

For us, Jesus is OUR Promised Land...
We can enter Heaven through Him!!!

*Have **YOU** accepted this AMAZING gift?*

042

'God Has Made A Way'

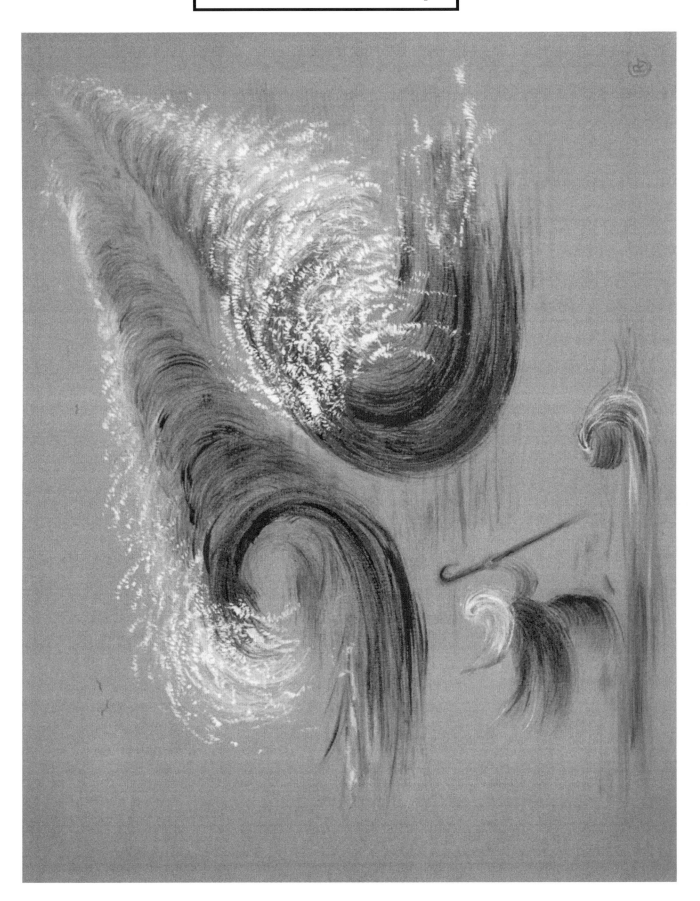

'God Has Made A Way'

'Jesus said, "I AM the Way, the Truth and the Life, no one comes to the Father except through me."' (John 14:6)

Date: ___ / ___ / _____ To: _____ From: _____

A colouring gift from Me to You...taken from the book:

CHRISTIAN COLOURING BOOK **LARGE PRINT** DEVOTIONAL...*and more!!!* (Volume 1)

By **ART THAT SPEAKS** – Rita Clark (*found on Amazon*)

Painting 13: **'There's Always Hope'**

About the Painting...

I initially started this painting using lime green and dark blue. I can't remember exactly what I was trying to achieve, but I do remember being frustrated with the result. So I exclaimed to God, *"You'll have to do this Lord!"* ...and with that, I started blocking-out my canvas with a dusky-pink acrylic mix. I paused to ponder and trusted that the Lord would help me. By faith I was certain that the painting I hoped for, would eventually materialise. In that moment, I was reminded of an avenue of trees I had once considered painting. I felt warmed in my heart. *Yes...that is what I would paint!* My avenue would lead into the light. The dusky-pink would be my morning sky that hosted the rising sunlight. The sunlight would represent Jesus...*the Light of the world!* And my avenue would be the path leading into His presence. I felt satisfied; I began to paint, and this was the result.

Thoughts to Ponder...

I think I chose 'There's Always Hope' as the title, because by faith God can turn any disaster into something hopeful. In fact, I have often used this particular painting when telling my own salvation story. In 1986, when my circumstances were very different, Jesus met me at the point of my deepest need. As I reached out to this unknown God, He spoke to me in an audible voice. In that moment, I knew God was real and that He loved me...*see my testimony on page 101.*

God longs to meet with YOU; He wants to meet you at your point of need, however great or small. Why not let the sunlight of His presence fill you? In Jesus, 'There's Always Hope'.

The Bible says in Matthew 11, verse 28, *'Come to Me, all you who are weary and burdened, and I will give you rest'.*

He loves YOU and beckons you 'Come'...will you?

'There's Always Hope'

'Come to Me, all you who are weary and burdened,
and I will give you rest'. **(Matthew 11:28)**

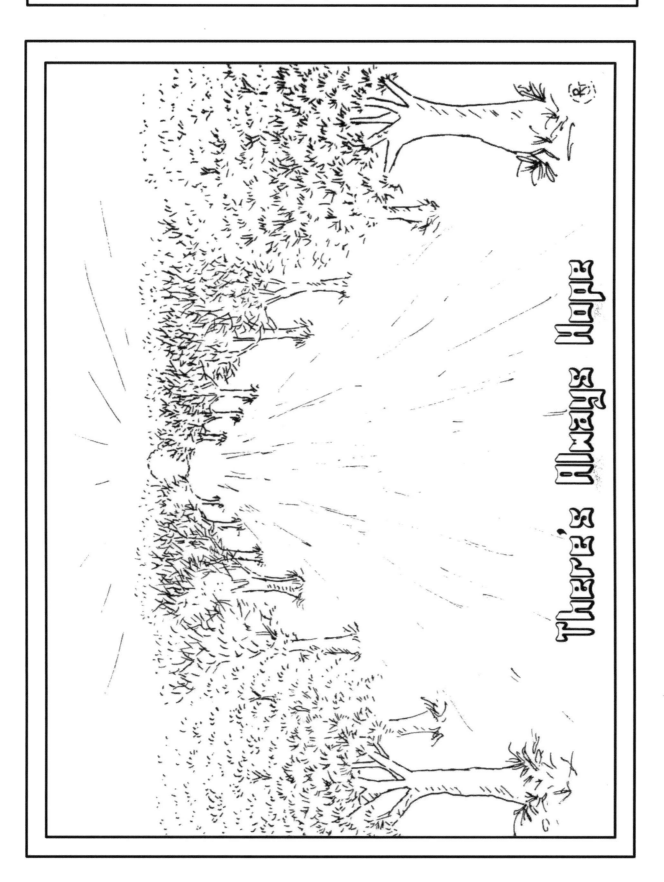

There's Always Hope

Date: ___ / ___ / _____ To: _____ From: _____

A colouring gift from Me to You...taken from the book:

CHRISTIAN COLOURING BOOK **LARGE PRINT** DEVOTIONAL...*and more!!!* (Volume 1)

By **ART THAT SPEAKS** – Rita Clark (*found on Amazon*)

Painting 12: **'Weeping'**

About the Painting...

In an art workshop I once attended, the tutor asked the group, "How does God feel about your failure?" The very first image that entered my mind was me as a child, cowering before my shouting, alcoholic father. But because I was now a Christian and knew the love of God, I immediately pushed that ugly picture from my mind and exclaimed, *"NO! – that's NOT how my Heavenly Father would treat me!"* In my mind's eye, I saw myself as a child run into the arms of God and felt the warmth of His tears weeping over me...*so that's the image I painted!*

Thoughts to Ponder...

With this painting, I wanted to concentrate on the compassion of God...*and His amazing love for each one of us individually!* In the Bible, in John 11 verse 35, it says, *'Jesus wept'.* He was moved with compassion and shed tears, when He saw Mary weeping for her brother Lazarus, who had died. I'm convinced that God identifies with OUR pain and weeps with us *in OUR brokenness...*

I believe that's 'How God sees my failure'...*and I'm convinced that's how God sees YOUR failure too!!!*

In your heart, why not take a moment right now,
and run into His welcoming, ever-open arms?

Let Him embrace you...He loves you!!!

'Weeping'

He was moved with compassion and shed tears.
'Jesus wept'   *(John 11:35)*

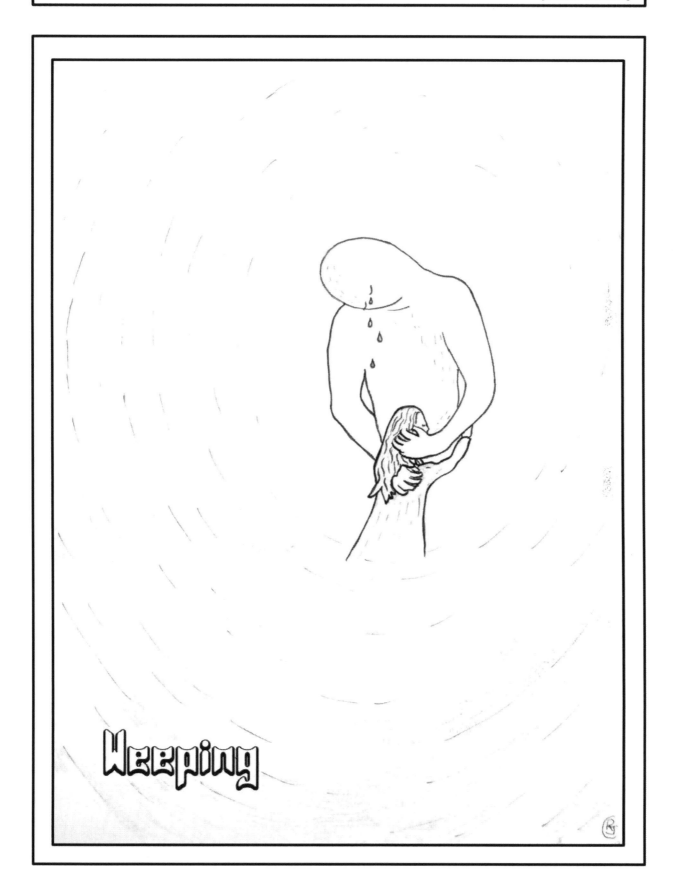

Date: ___ / ___ / _____ To: _____ From: _____

A colouring gift from Me to You...taken from the book:

CHRISTIAN COLOURING BOOK **LARGE PRINT** DEVOTIONAL...*and more!!!* (Volume 1)

By **ART THAT SPEAKS** – Rita Clark (*found on Amazon*)

Painting 14: **'Step Into Hope'**

About the Painting...

Heather, a friend in her 70's, had just lost her long-time sweetheart...*he had gone to be with The Lord.* My heart went out to her – *now she'd have to do life alone...* Looking back however, I think that reflected the sadness *in my heart* rather than hers! Nonetheless, they were the thoughts that inspired the painting. Thankfully, Heather knows how to place her hope in Jesus...*He is her strength!*

The sadness in my heart wanted Heather to look to the future with hope. So, I decided to make 'HOPE' the focal point of my painting. As I thought about this, the hardy shrub heather came to mind...*her namesake!* In my mind's eye I saw a beautiful but barren mauve terrain, with a mountain range in the distance. This seemed perfect as I wanted to express both bleakness *and* hope! I love featuring sunsets whenever I can...*to me personally they're an expression of hope!* When I see a sunset, *I experience God's loving arms around me!* A gentle path leading through the word 'HOPE', and then heading off towards an atmospheric sunset, somehow captured *everything* I wanted to say!!!

Thoughts to Ponder...

The Bible says in Romans 15, verse 13, '*May the God of Hope fill you with all joy and peace as you trust in Him, so that you may overflow with hope by the power of the Holy Spirit.'*

'Step Into Hope'...allow YOUR heart to overflow with peace and joy, as you place YOUR trust in Jesus!

HE is the hope YOUR heart searches for!!!

Step Into Hope

'*May the God of Hope fill you with all joy and peace as you trust in Him, so that you may overflow with hope by the power of the Holy Spirit.*' *(Romans 15:13)*

Date: ___ / ___ / _____ To: _____ From: _____

A colouring gift from Me to You...taken from the book:

CHRISTIAN COLOURING BOOK **LARGE PRINT** DEVOTIONAL...*and more!!!* (Volume 1)

By **ART THAT SPEAKS** – Rita Clark (*found on Amazon*)

Painting 15: 'The Lord Is My Shepherd'

About the Painting...

For me, the gentle colours and soft movement in this painting, express the deep sense of peace I feel whenever I hear Psalm 23 read. In verses 1-3a it says, '*The Lord is my shepherd; I shall not be in want. He makes me lie down in green pastures; He leads me beside quiet waters; He restores my soul.*' The Lord – my Shepherd – *IS my cup of refreshing that overflows!*

As a child, each time I heard these words read in my school assembly, they would bring great comfort. In those moments I could escape from my little world of heartache, insecurities, fears, and my dad's alcoholic behaviour. Looking back, I now realise that in those moments, I sensed the closeness of God and the hope of a better tomorrow. *God IS faithful!!!*

Thoughts to Ponder...

Apart from that childhood experience, there have been two other significant events in my life, where God used Psalm 23 to impart His Life to my soul. One was a vision *(see my testimony on page 104)* and the other was where His voice spoke the reassurance and comfort I would need *to carry me through imminent great loss...*

Perhaps you're familiar with this Psalm yourself and have fond memories of it – *you can be reminded of the words on page 077.* Why not stop for a few moments? Consider HIS words of comfort toward YOU...*right now!!!*

Allow God's peace to wash over you...
He longs to touch YOU with His Spirit!!!

'The Lord Is My Shepherd'

'*The Lord is my shepherd; I shall not be in want. He makes me lie down in green pastures; He leads me beside quiet waters; He restores my soul.*' (Psalm 23:1-3a)

Date: ___ / ___ / _____ To: _____ From: _____

A colouring gift from Me to You...taken from the book:

CHRISTIAN COLOURING BOOK **LARGE PRINT** DEVOTIONAL...*and more!!!* (Volume 1)

By **ART THAT SPEAKS** – Rita Clark (*found on Amazon*)

Painting 16: **'Walking With Jesus'**
(*'The Long Road Home'* by Louise Clark)

About the Painting...

Whenever I use this painting in the ministry of Art That Speaks, I call it 'Walking With Jesus'. My daughter Louise, who painted it, calls it *'The Long Road Home'*. She painted it as an act of worship to express her gratitude to God. After many years of pain, having grown up with an absent father, she suddenly, in a moment, *broke free!* In that instant, she made Jesus her Lord and Saviour. *This is how she describes her profound experience...*

"So then, the beginning of my new life can be marked by one single moment, but a moment that will last until the end; all in one simple, yet terrifyingly-powerful revelation from God – I understood...**He is my dad!**   Everything I ever thought I needed; the means to mend my broken heart; everything I thought I'd spent the last 19 years without – *I'd had it all along!!!"*

Thoughts to Ponder...

The moment Louise looked to Jesus to fill that great empty void in her soul, she found freedom from pain and loss. She had searched in many wrong places to meet that need when Jesus was walking by her side *the whole time!!!*

"Then you will know the truth & the truth will set you free."
"So if the Son sets you free, you will be free indeed."
(John 8, verses 32 & 36 from the Bible)

Has your heart already found rest and salvation in Jesus?
If it hasn't...*it's NOT TOO LATE!!!*

God invites YOU to walk with His Son.

Will YOU invite Jesus into your life TODAY???

'Walking With Jesus'

'Then you will know the truth & the truth will set you free.'
'So if the Son sets you free, you will be free indeed.'

(John 8:32 & 36)

Date: ___ / ___ / _____ To: _____ From: _____

A colouring gift from Me to You...taken from the book:

CHRISTIAN COLOURING BOOK **LARGE PRINT** DEVOTIONAL...*and more!!!* (Volume 1)

By **ART THAT SPEAKS** – Rita Clark (*found on Amazon*)

Section 2

Pictures with Scriptures!

In this section there are 16 pictures with scriptures for you to meditate on whilst colouring. To help you, I've tried to create simple pictures and have avoided anything too intricate or complicated. That way, you won't have to think too hard about your colouring experience and can set your heart fully on fellowship with God. It is my heart's prayer that you will draw closer to God through each section of this colouring book.

Incidentally, don't forget there are 'CUT LINES' on each picture so they can be detached and framed if you would like to do so. Why keep them hidden? Why not give them the opportunity to be a blessing to all who see them, *INCLUDING YOURSELF?* Alternatively, you may like to give them as gifts to others, to encourage them...

Remember – Enjoy and LET GOD SPEAK!!!

Only Believe...

Based on: Mark 5:36

Date: ___ / ___ / _____ To: _____ From: _____

A colouring gift from Me to You...taken from the book:

CHRISTIAN COLOURING BOOK **LARGE PRINT** DEVOTIONAL...*and more!!!* (Volume 1)

By **ART THAT SPEAKS** – Rita Clark (*found on Amazon*)

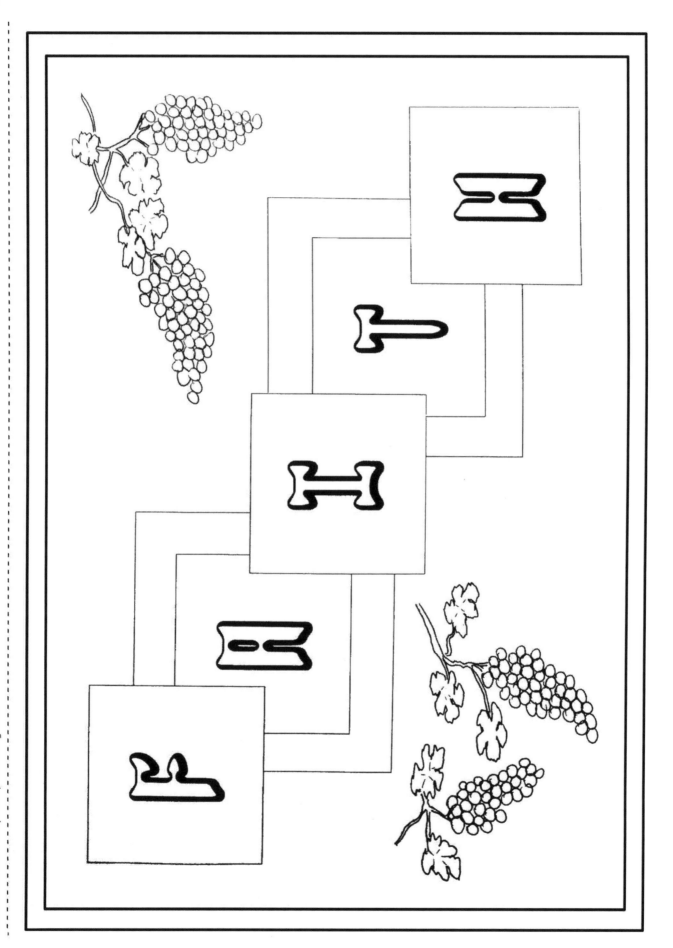

Date: ___ / ___ / _____ To: _____ From: _____

A colouring gift from Me to You...taken from the book:

CHRISTIAN COLOURING BOOK **LARGE PRINT** DEVOTIONAL...*and more!!!* (Volume 1)

By **ART THAT SPEAKS** – Rita Clark (*found on Amazon*)

Date: ___ / ___ / _____ To: _____ From: _____

A colouring gift from Me to You...taken from the book:

CHRISTIAN COLOURING BOOK **LARGE PRINT** DEVOTIONAL...*and more!!!* (Volume 1)

By **ART THAT SPEAKS** – Rita Clark (*found on Amazon*)

073

Jesus Is The Truth...

Based on: John 14:6

Date: ____ / ____ / _____ To: _____ From: _____

A colouring gift from Me to You...taken from the book:

CHRISTIAN COLOURING BOOK **LARGE PRINT** DEVOTIONAL....*and more!!!* (Volume 1)

By **ART THAT SPEAKS** – Rita Clark (*found on Amazon*)

Date: ___ / ___ / _____ To: _____ From: _____

A colouring gift from Me to You...taken from the book:

CHRISTIAN COLOURING BOOK **LARGE PRINT** DEVOTIONAL...*and more!!!* (Volume 1)

By **ART THAT SPEAKS** – Rita Clark (*found on Amazon*)

Psalm 23

The LORD *is* my shepherd;
I shall not want.
He makes me lie down
in green pastures,
He leads me beside still waters;
He restores my soul.
He leads me in the paths
of righteousness,
for His name's sake.
Even though I walk through the valley
of the shadow of death,
I will fear no evil;
For You *are* with me;
Your rod and Your staff,
they comfort me.
You prepare a table before me,
in the presence of my enemies.
You anoint my head with oil;
My cup overflows.
Surely goodness and mercy,
shall follow me
all the days of my life;
And I will dwell in the house of
The LORD forever.

Date: ___ / ___ / _____ To: _____ From: _____

A colouring gift from Me to You...taken from the book:

CHRISTIAN COLOURING BOOK **LARGE PRINT** DEVOTIONAL...*and more!!!* (Volume 1)

By **ART THAT SPEAKS** – Rita Clark (*found on Amazon*)

Be Reconciled To God Through Christ...

Based on: 2 Corinthians 5:20

Date: ___ / ___ / _____ To: _____ From: _____

A colouring gift from Me to You...taken from the book:

CHRISTIAN COLOURING BOOK **LARGE PRINT** DEVOTIONAL...*and more!!!* (Volume 1)

By **ART THAT SPEAKS** – Rita Clark (*found on Amazon*)

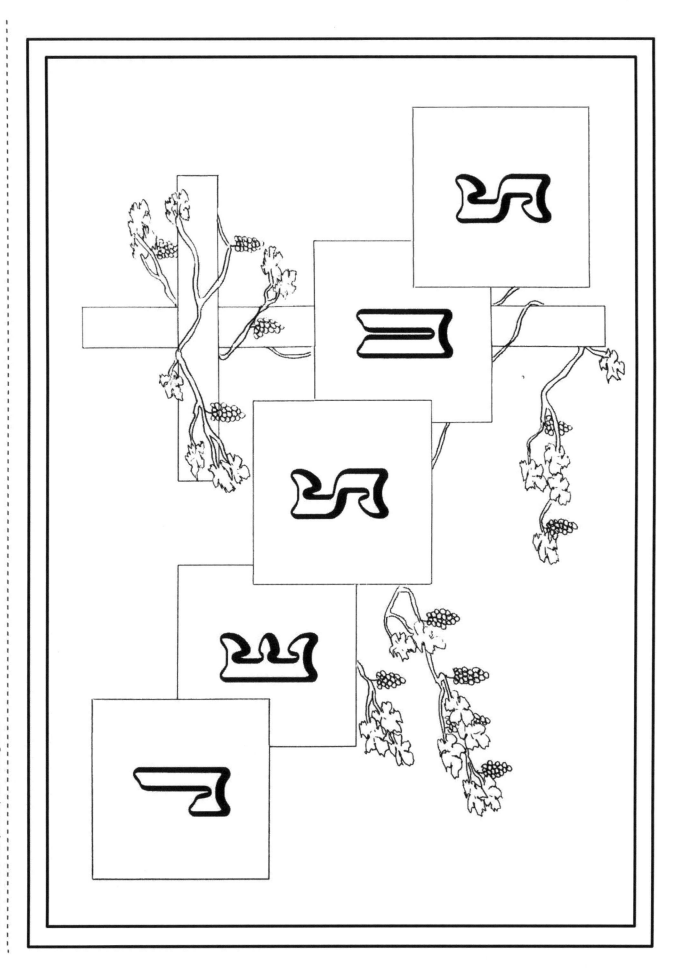

Date: ___ / ___ / _____ To: _____ From: _____

A colouring gift from Me to You...taken from the book:

CHRISTIAN COLOURING BOOK **LARGE PRINT** DEVOTIONAL...*and more!!!* (Volume 1)

By **ART THAT SPEAKS** – Rita Clark (*found on Amazon*)

All Things Are Possible For The One Who Believes!!!

Based on: Mark 9:23

Date: ____ / ____ / _____ To: _____ From: _____

A colouring gift from Me to You...taken from the book:

CHRISTIAN COLOURING BOOK **LARGE PRINT** DEVOTIONAL...*and more!!!* (Volume 1)

By **ART THAT SPEAKS** – Rita Clark (*found on Amazon*)

Jesus Is The Life...

Based on: John 14:6

Date: ___ / ___ / _____ To: _____ From: _____

A colouring gift from Me to You...taken from the book:

CHRISTIAN COLOURING BOOK **LARGE PRINT** DEVOTIONAL...*and more!!!* (Volume 1)

By **ART THAT SPEAKS** – Rita Clark (*found on Amazon*)

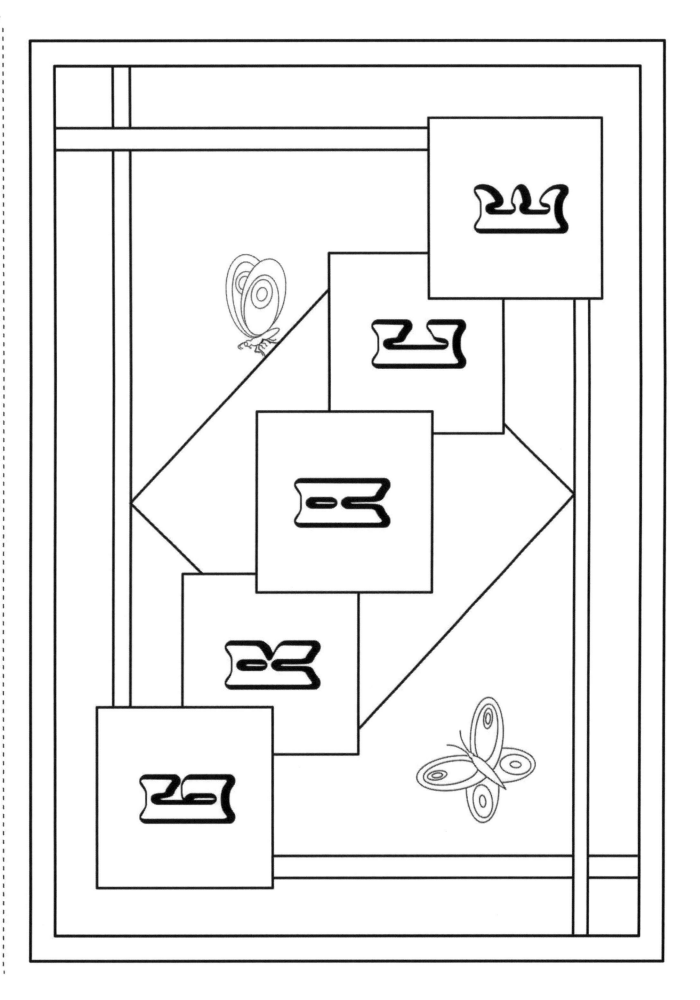

Date: ___ / ___ / _____ To: _____ From: _____

A colouring gift from Me to You...taken from the book:

CHRISTIAN COLOURING BOOK **LARGE PRINT** DEVOTIONAL...*and more!!!* (Volume 1)

By **ART THAT SPEAKS** – Rita Clark (*found on Amazon*)

Based on: Ephesians 2:8

By Grace Through Faith

Date: ___ / ___ / _____ To: _____ From: _____

A colouring gift from Me to You...taken from the book:

CHRISTIAN COLOURING BOOK **LARGE PRINT** DEVOTIONAL...*and more!!!* (Volume 1)

By **ART THAT SPEAKS** – Rita Clark (*found on Amazon*)

In HIM was Life,
and the Life
was the Light
of Men

Based on: John 1:4

Date: ___ / ___ / _____ To: _____ From: _____

A colouring gift from Me to You...taken from the book:

CHRISTIAN COLOURING BOOK **LARGE PRINT** DEVOTIONAL...*and more!!!* (Volume 1)

By **ART THAT SPEAKS** – Rita Clark (*found on Amazon*)

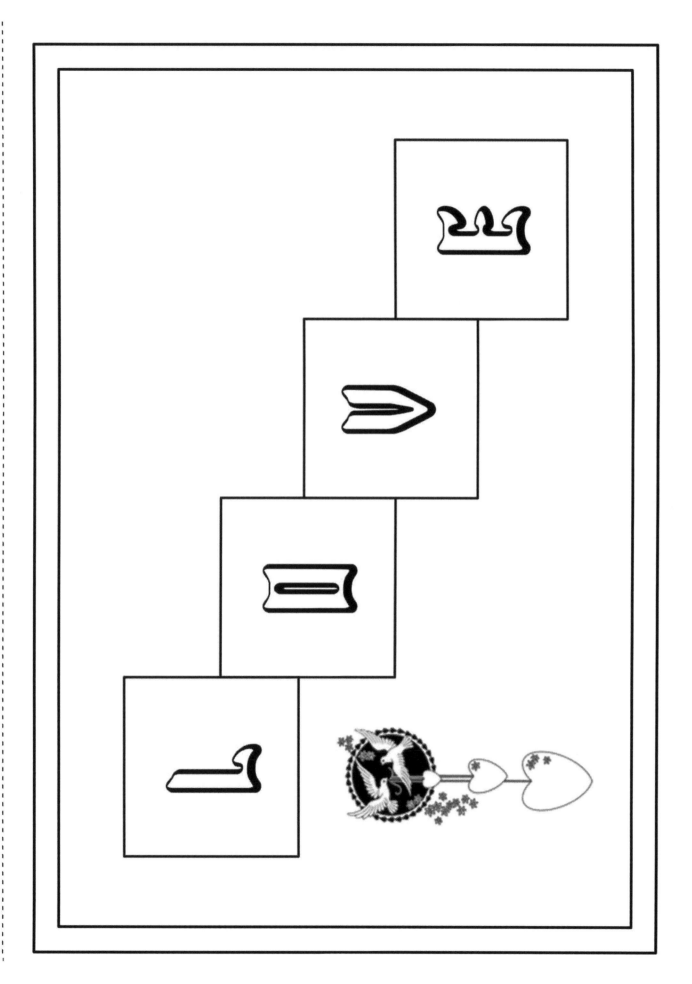

Date: ___ / ___ / _____ To: _____ From: _____

A colouring gift from Me to You...taken from the book:

CHRISTIAN COLOURING BOOK **LARGE PRINT** DEVOTIONAL...*and more!!!* (Volume 1)

By **ART THAT SPEAKS** – Rita Clark (*found on Amazon*)

Just Receive...

Based on: John 20:22

Date: ___ / ___ / _____ To: _____ From: _____

A colouring gift from Me to You...taken from the book:

CHRISTIAN COLOURING BOOK **LARGE PRINT** DEVOTIONAL...*and more!!!* (Volume 1)

By **ART THAT SPEAKS** – Rita Clark (*found on Amazon*)

The Lord's Prayer

Our Father, who art in heaven,
Hallowed be Thy name;
Thy kingdom come;
Thy will be done;
on earth as it is in heaven.
Give us this day our daily bread.
And forgive us our trespasses,
as we forgive those who trespass
against us.
And lead us not into temptation;
but deliver us from evil.
For Thine is the kingdom,
the power and the glory,
for ever and ever.
Amen.

Date: ___ / ___ / _____ To: _____ From: _____

A colouring gift from Me to You...taken from the book:

CHRISTIAN COLOURING BOOK **LARGE PRINT** DEVOTIONAL...*and more!!!* (Volume 1)

By **ART THAT SPEAKS** – Rita Clark (*found on Amazon*)

Section 3

Testimonies
Invitation & Prayer
Blessing
Dedications
Art That Speaks
Books

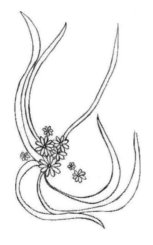

Jesus and Sunsets

God's Voice...

In several of my write-ups in this colouring book, I've mentioned hearing the *audible voice of God* and my love of sunsets! So, rather than leaving this hanging in mid-air, I thought it would be good to explain what happened. Also, to make sense of the story, I feel it's necessary to mention my ex-husband. However, it's important to point out that we are good friends now, despite the past. The goodness and grace of God have even covered the events surrounding that; *I've TOTALLY forgiven him!!!*

About Me...

The short version of my story is that I didn't know God; I'd been raised in a faithless home with an alcoholic father and a mother who often lay in bed steeped in depression. I became conditioned to thinking that this oppressive atmosphere was 'normal'. It was the only way of life I knew, and it slowly became engrained in me. It shaped who I was and my expectation of what life could offer me.

Deep in my heart I hungered for the reality of God. I'd heard the story of Jesus *'feeding the five thousand'* when I was in Primary School. I'd also heard the words of Psalm 23 read in school assembly, *'The Lord is my Shepherd',* and this *always* touched me deeply. But that was it; I had no *real* understanding of God or who He was.

Continued...

The Nightmare...

In 1986, my first and only child was born via C-section. I knew *NOTHING* about motherhood, and my body screamed with exhaustion from the surgery. I was told I'd have to rest for three months – *but with a new-born baby that was impossible!!!* To make matters worse, I had just moved home (and district) two months earlier, was still living out of tea chests, and everything was a shamble. Then my dog died, and my husband bought a puppy which kept *ME* awake for many nights! *Life was like swimming in treacle...* And if *that* wasn't enough, my alcoholic husband frequently failed to come home at night. Then, when he did, he would often provoke a bitter argument and leave again! All of this led me into fear, hopelessness, and a state of deep suicidal depression. I hid myself away, riddled with shame, *and felt totally isolated...*

The Christening...

In my new village setting I decided to take myself off to church, as I wanted my daughter, Louise, christened. However, the vicar told me before he could do that I'd have to be christened and confirmed myself. This seemed a little strange but I agreed anyway. I'm not sure why...*but it felt like the right thing to do!*

The vicar started to teach me the things of God in preparation for my confirmation. Everything went over my head; I just did what I was told. But, one day, in my suicidal swamp called life, I unwittingly questioned God with the only words that had wedged themselves into my subconsciousness: *"How can I love you with all my heart, with all my soul, and with all my mind? I need to feel someone's arms around me!"* (If you recall my husband was hardly ever home.) Then, the most amazing thing happened, and it changed my life forever – *I heard the audible voice of God!!!*

God spoke...

"How do you feel when you walk across the open fields?" "I feel good", I said. *"How do you feel when you see the sunset?"* "I feel good", I said again. *"How do you feel when you see your baby smile?"* And again I said, "I feel good", *"THIS is how I put my arms around you..."* And with that, what I can only describe as an incredible power, full of love, surged through my entire body, from the top of my head to the soles of my feet. It was like someone pulled a plug from my toes and the suicidal depression poured out – *I KNEW God was real!!!*

The Embrace...

There is more to this story; however, it's sufficient to say this is the reason I love to paint both Jesus and sunsets. When I thought I was isolated and alone, *God was ALWAYS there!* Creation itself expresses the nature of God; He used nature to put His arms around and embrace me. That explains why I always felt hugged in the big outdoors...*and still do!!!*

Think about that... You may not hear His audible voice and you're probably not staring into a sunset, *but God is always speaking...* He gives to each one of us *exactly* what He knows our heart needs!!!

He is ALWAYS present!
He is with YOU right now!!
Embracing YOU in His arms!!!
Will you invite Him to hug you closer?

The Lord is My Shepherd

Psalm 23

An Important Psalm...

As a child I would often hear Psalm 23 read in the school assembly. As I listened it would touch my heart deeply...*every time!* I knew when I reached the fourth-year, I would eventually get the opportunity to read a passage of my choice. For four years, I savoured in my heart that I could read Psalm 23 myself, and now – aged 11 and about to leave primary school – *my time was finally approaching...*

I was afraid to get up on that big stage in front of the whole school. So afraid in fact, my teacher allowed me to be the last to read in our class of over forty kids. I had learning difficulties at the time and struggled with reading. I practiced and practiced, and *eventually* my big, beautiful, yet terrifying day arrived! *In trepidation and fear I mounted the stage... 'You were too fast!!!'* the teacher hissed at me as I left the stage. *A sword pierced my heart, I had failed...*

Time Stood Still...

About thirty years later, having been a Christian roughly seven years, I was in a back room of the church worshipping The Lord with a friend. She had put on worship music from a CD and I suddenly heard the song, *'The Lord Is My Shepherd'* being played.

In that moment time stood still and I entered a vision...

It was as if I had been transported. I instantly found myself looking into an *immensely bright light!* As gazed at the centre of the light, I saw a person and suddenly realised *it was me!!!* I was just eleven years old again and standing back on that same stage in my school assembly. *Then I heard The Lord speak... "I see your heart!!!"*

I snapped back into the natural realm and knew immediately that I was changed. God showed me I hadn't really failed in His sight at all. HE had seen my heart...*and HE was pleased with me!!!*

It Was Gone...

All the years I'd carried the pain that had broken my heart – *in a moment it was gone!!!* It didn't matter anymore that I was *'too fast'*. No! God was with me then – *even though I didn't realise it* – and had seen my heart! *And God is with me now!* He WAS and IS pleased with me...*and that is ALL that matters!!!*

––––––––––––––––––

Think about that for a moment...*what does that mean for you?* Let me tell you something; you may not realise it, but God has also been with YOU – *every moment of YOUR life!*

And He's STILL with you RIGHT NOW...
HE LOVES YOU!!!

He has NEVER stopped loving you...
And He NEVER will!!!

Nan's Story – *It's Not Too Late!!!*

Something Happened...

I sat next to Nan in her hospital bed. She was about to die, and I was concerned...*she didn't appear to know Jesus as her Lord and Saviour!*

'I was in the Salvation Army', Nan informed me. This totally surprised me...*but was good to hear!* She then listed all the wonderful things she'd done that assured her she'd be 'ok' for when *that final moment* came! However, I told her 'good works' – as good as they may be – *wouldn't get her into Heaven!!!* Only accepting the shed blood of Jesus Christ as payment for her sin would guarantee her access.

'Can I pray for you Nan?', I asked. She avoided the question, so I asked again. 'You'll have to ask Charlie', she said (that was her son who'd lived with her all his life). I said again, 'No Nan, I'm asking you!' But now she was getting frustrated by my audacity to ask. She pushed it back again and said, 'Ask Charlie', 'No Nan, I'm asking you!' Finally, in frustration – and probably to get rid of me – with a huff, she agreed. *So, I started to pray...*

Angels Sang...

'I can hear angels singing', Nan exclaimed! I was flabbergasted, I couldn't hear a thing! 'What are they singing?', I asked her. *'Jesus wants me for a sunbeam'*, she replied. I left the hospital that day on cloud nine...*but was it enough???*

A few days later I returned...

I walked into the room with my 8-year-old daughter and sister Linda. If I recall correctly, there were eight of us around the bed that day; this was rather disappointing as I'd hoped to speak more with Nan about Jesus. But alas, it was too late*...or so I thought!* Nan had now lost her mind and was talking of nothing but oranges! She also insisted on playing a game of 'Postman' with us the whole time we were there! Back and forth we went, one at a time, as Nan repeatedly thrust her get-well-soon cards at us, for us to then deliver back to her!!!

I left that day with a heavy heart; I'd missed it – I couldn't be sure Nan was saved. BUT, *she had heard the angels singing to her...I had to trust God!!!*

The Next Visit...

I went back yet again to visit Nan; this time I took my Mum with me so she could say her own farewell. I felt a bit awkward; I desperately wanted to talk to Nan about her salvation, but here I was with Mum who didn't yet know Jesus herself. I struggled with taking her but what could I do? *Her own mother was about to die!* So there we both were, sitting at Nan's bedside.

Nan started to hiss at me, which scared me somewhat...

Mum started to laugh, she thought it was funny! I didn't; I knew in my heart what the cause was...*so I held my ground.* Sadly, Nan was still confused and spoke of nothing but oranges for the next hour. Finally, it was time for us to leave as I had to pick my daughter up from school. But then, totally unexpectedly, I heard myself ask, 'Nan, can I pray for you?' And when she said 'Yes', *I was completely shocked!* Remember, Nan was out of her mind...*yet she agreed!!!*

Continued...

I Prayed...

I bowed my head to pray and said, 'Dear Lord Jesus'...*I didn't have a clue where I was going with this!* Suddenly, and very clearly, Nan said, *'Dear Lord Jesus!'* I WAS AMAZED!!! So I spoke again and Nan repeated my words. *I was even MORE stunned than before!* I can't remember *everything* I prayed that day, but I do remember that *Nan repeated EVERYTHING I SAID!!!* Somehow, I felt strangely detached from what was happening. Though I could still hear my voice continuing to pray, it seemed like I was watching a game of tennis, with words being batted back and forth between us. *It was surreal...*

I knew for sure I'd invited Jesus to be her Lord and Saviour – *and she definitely repeated that!* I was shocked...*but kept on speaking!* 'Amen', I said finally. *'Amen'*, Nan responded. And with that, this woman who moments before was behaving crazily and hissing at me, reached forward, grabbed me, dragged me towards her...*AND KISSED ME!!!* She had *NEVER* kissed me before *in my whole life!!!*

She then went back to talking about oranges and seemed oblivious to our presence, so at that point we got up to leave. I was still stunned! Wide-eyed, I turned to Mum and said, *'NAN IS GOING TO HEAVEN!!!'* As we left the hospital...*my heart overflowed with rejoicing!*

Heaven Bound...

God is sooooo wonderful!!! He knew Nan had served Him with the best of her ability, so He came to claim her as His own in her last hour. She had served Him in her own strength, believing in her own good works, but they of themselves weren't enough. She needed to receive Jesus as her personal Lord and Saviour; the only way she could do this was to exchange her *own* works for the finished work of the cross. Jesus alone paid the price for Nan's sin.

A Special Invitation!

Have you placed YOUR trust in Jesus?

Perhaps you're reading this because He wants to

give YOU the opportunity to come to Him!

Will you accept Him as your personal Saviour?

This is YOUR moment!!!

Why not respond NOW???

Ephesians 2:8-9

'For it is by grace you have been saved,

through faith – and this is not from yourselves,

*it is the gift of God – **not by works**,*

so that none can boast.'

John 6:29

'Jesus said "This is the work of God, that you

***believe in Him** whom He has sent."'*

To understand more about how to have a relationship with Jesus, please see page 110

Invitation and Prayer

In the Beginning...

Perhaps this colouring book was a gift from a friend, or it came into your possession by other means. Possibly, your colouring experience or my stories in this book, caused you to realise that God really does exist; you now know He loves you and wants ***a personal relationship with YOU!!!*** I'd love to take this opportunity to tell you something about Jesus Christ, God's Son, and how to receive Him as your personal Saviour. The Bible tells us in John 14, verse 6, '*Jesus said, "I AM the Way, the Truth and the Life, no-one comes to the Father except through ME."'* Therefore, it is my heartfelt hope that this colouring book will guide you into a loving relationship with God Himself.

The Bible is God's manual for life and gives us the purpose for our very existence. It tells us the story of redemption, through the shed blood of Jesus on the cross, more than 2000 years ago. It explains why Jesus came to earth; about His death, burial and resurrection; and how His perfect sacrifice can restore us to a relationship with Father God. It is that restored relationship into which I now invite you...

In the beginning, man was created for relationship with God, but through disobedience that relationship was broken (the Bible calls this 'sin'). You can read the full account of creation and mankind in Genesis, the first book of the Bible. To understand the fullness of what that means for you personally, it would be helpful to read the account for yourself.

In the Bible, God tells us if we seek Him with *ALL* our heart, *we **WILL** find Him!* I can absolutely promise you that this is TRUE. It just needs your **whole heart** to reach out to Him. There are no magical words to say and no rules and regulations. You don't need to be living a perfect life – be it organised or a complete mess – *you just need to realise your need and come as you are!*

He **WILL** hear and He **WILL** answer! It may not be an audible voice, but I guarantee you will KNOW for sure He's heard you. ***He WILL make Himself known to you!!!***

In the Bible, in John 3, verses 16 & 17, it says, *'For God so loved the world that He gave His one and only Son, so that **WHOEVER** believes in Him will not die but will have eternal life. For God did not send His Son into the world to condemn the world, but that the world through Him might be saved.'*

As an act of faith, let me encourage you to choose, believe and receive Jesus as your personal Saviour. Father God promises, *in that very moment,* **YOU WILL** become His child. *Your eternal life begins immediately!* Then, as you grow in the knowledge of Him and ALL He has for you, you'll learn how to receive *His peace*, peace that passes all understanding. You will now have found the very thing **YOU** were created for – *an everlasting relationship with God!*

God has given you FREE WILL. Here is your opportunity, your invitation, to start a new life with Jesus today. Will you do that? ***I promise you'll be so glad you did!*** *If you are wondering how to do this, there is a simple guide to help you on the next page.*

*Remember, there are no special words…it just needs your **whole heart** to reach out to Him!!!*

Suggested Guide for Prayer...

In the Bible, in Romans 10, verses 9 & 10, it says:

'If you declare with your mouth, 'Jesus is Lord', and believe in your heart that God raised him from the dead, you will be saved. For it is with your heart that you believe and are justified, and it is with your mouth that you profess your faith and are saved.'

Just speak to God (we call this 'prayer'), acknowledge that Jesus died for you on the cross, was buried, and rose from the grave! Then, ask His forgiveness for your own personal sin (wrongdoing)...*and thank Him!* Use your own words – you can't get it wrong – **God looks at your heart!!!**

Alternatively, you could speak this prayer:

'Jesus, I confess You as my Lord. I believe in my heart You died for my sin and that God raised You from the dead. Therefore, I believe that by faith I am saved. Thank you for saving me, Amen.'

Hallelujah! Let me be the first to welcome you into God's family. You can be assured that God will be with you to lead and guide you into all Truth, with the help of His Holy Spirit.

If a friend gave you this colouring book, please let them know what you've done and ask for their guidance on the best way forward. Whatever you do...***don't remain alone!*** You belong to a bigger family now – *God's family!* Please remember to share your new-found joy!!!

YOUR life is PRECIOUS!!! The Bible tells us the angels in heaven rejoice over one sinner who comes to Jesus. Please *feel free* to contact me to let me know if, for the **very first time**, you have asked Jesus into your life. *It would be such a blessing to hear your news and share heaven's joy!*

Thank you and God bless you, Rita

If you would like to contact me, please do so via:

Email: rita.artthatspeaks@gmail.com

(Alternatively, it would be great to shake your hand in heaven, when each of us eventually arrive there...)

"The LORD bless you
and keep you;
the LORD make His
Face shine on you
and be gracious to you;
the LORD
turn His Face
toward you
and give you peace"

I guess I'm a bit unconventional putting DEDICATIONS
at the back of this book!
However, as I have the FREEDOM to be ME,
that's the way I've chosen to do it!

DEDICATIONS

'Nanny Parker' – Anne Jane Isabel Parker
20/07/1901 to 19/10/1994 (aged 93)

I'd like to dedicate this colouring book to my Nan...*and to honour all who have gone before!!!* They have a special place in our hearts, and we cherish their memory despite the passage of time. We recall their presence in our lives with warmth and affection.

———————————————————

I'd also like to dedicate this Colouring Book to my daughter Louise who, back in December 2005, exclaimed, *"MOTHER, YOU MUST PAINT!!!"* so in obedience and trepidation, I set aside 28th December 2005 as a day to paint. On that momentous day, I created my first four paintings on a used canvas and some old pieces of hardboard. In 2006, 'ART THAT SPEAKS' was birthed out of this command. I am extremely grateful for her tough words; they broke the back of my haunting fear and launched me not only into the joy of painting, but also this ministry.

I'm also grateful to my long-standing friend Keith, who has tirelessly stuck with me over the years as general supporter, encourager, laptop keeper, editor, sounding-board, and prayer warrior. Thank you for your patience, and for giving up so much of your precious time...*I think there have been many occasions when that patience was somewhat tried!!!*

My thanks to you both, I hope you are blessed by my achievements!

And, of course, my greatest thanks to the Lord Himself...

Thank You Father!!!

Art That Speaks uses the creative gift of art to open people's hearts and minds to the love of God. God's touch, released through the unthreatening medium of art, can bring faith, hope, healing, encouragement, restoration and salvation to young and old alike.

If you are using any of my books for **OUTREACH PURPOSES** and would like my **PDF** of the simple **SURVEY** I use to assist with your own outreach endeavours, please feel free to contact me:

Email: **rita.artthatspeaks@gmail.com**
Subject: **PDF SURVEY REQUEST**

For useful **COLOURING TIPS** and to see my own personal work, please follow me on **INSTAGRAM @ rita.artthatspeaks**

To locate further ART THAT SPEAKS books:

- Enter the ISBN number of **THIS** book into the Amazon Search Bar.
- Select book – the Book Title and Details will appear.
- Below the **Book Title** you will see links to **Author** & **Contributor**.
- Click on **Art That Speaks** (Author) to see further books in collection.
- Click on **Books To Bless** (Contributor) to see <u>all</u> books published.

ISBN: 9798565010268
(UK SPELLING)

ISBN: 9798567130292
(USA SPELLING)

Volume 1 of this series has **5 sections** in the book. Section 1 has 12 greyscale pictures of my original art with drawings to colour. It also includes the inspiration behind the paintings, together with meditations to embrace. Sections 2 & 3 each contain prompts and several spaces/frames to encourage one's own personal creativity. Section 4 has 12 scripture drawings to colour. The final section includes a personal testimony/story, and an invitation & prayer. This Christian Colouring Book Devotional inspires a deeper relationship with God...*and is also an excellent outreach tool for those open to the Christian faith!!!*

IF you would like to AVOID duplication of drawings please purchase volumes within the SAME series, as and when they become available. To see the original art used within each book, please visit Amazon to look at the individual pictures on the back cover. – *See above to locate all books published.*

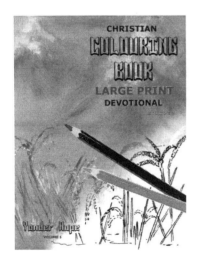

ISBN: 9798741026267
(UK SPELLING)

ISBN: 9798741032176
(USA SPELLING)

Volume 1 of this LARGE PRINT series has **3 sections** in the book with *clear, easy-to-read text!* Section 1 of this Christian Colouring Book Devotional has 16 greyscale pictures of my original art with drawings to colour. It also includes the inspiration behind the paintings, together with meditations to embrace. Section 2 has 16 scripture drawings to colour. Section 3 has three personal testimonies/stories, and an invitation & prayer. This book inspires a deeper relationship with God...*and is also an excellent outreach tool for those open to the Christian faith!!!*

IF you would like to AVOID duplication of drawings please purchase volumes within the SAME series, as and when they become available. To see the original art used within each book, please visit Amazon to look at the individual pictures on the back cover. – *See above to locate all books published.*

Printed in Great Britain
by Amazon